A Year in
Scrabo Country

David Kirk

Published by Cottage Publications,
an imprint of Laurel Cottage Ltd.
Donaghadee, N. Ireland 2014.

ISBN 978 1 900935 96 8

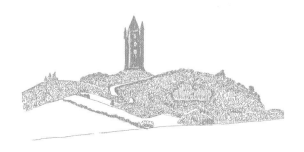

Contents

*To
Alana and Charles,
Simon and Charlotte,
for their help and support
in difficult times.*

David Kirk

Blue skies and dramatic clouds, deep glacial soils shaped into curving slopes giving well drained rich pastures – a scene that seems to sum up the unique personality of Scrabo Country

Man's life consists in a relation with all things – stone, earth, trees, flowers, water, insects, fishes, birds, all creatures

D H Lawrence

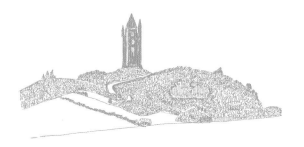

Introduction

No icy peaks reach for its skies, no water-falls thunder into deep ravines, few forest giants stride its slopes. Just a 500-foot hill, its iron-clad summit catching a drift of snow in a 'good' winter, and about 40 square miles of curvaceous pastoral landscape traced and explored by winding roads and clothed with the riches of one of the agriculturally most blessed parts of County Down.

Not in Scrabo Country the histrionics of the world's wild and high places, just a beauty to be found in the diversities of a gentle land bursting with exuberant life in summer, slumbering in winter – and always patterned by the ever changing patchwork of pasture and tillage.

Winter dawn light silhouettes Scrabo Hill and its dramatic tower

Scrabo Country's borders are marked on no map. It is a land of the mind and it welcomes and rewards all who seek out and enjoy the scenes of beauty and small dramas to be found in places all too often driven through without a glance – just taken for granted. A revelation awaits any who open their eyes and minds to them.

In fact the Scrabo Country that this work hopes to portray has no defined boundaries. Logically it could have included everywhere from which you can see Scrabo Tower – but that would have stretched as far as the Mourne Mountains! So it is roughly the countryside that could be said to be 'in the shadow' of the Hill – with a few forays outside it.

Newtownards, centre of the cultural and business life of the area, and now celebrating the beginning of its fifth century as a Royal Borough, thrives under the watchful eye of Scrabo Hill. It is Saturday morning and the heart of the town, Conway Square (bottom left) is patterned with the rings of stands at the open air market. Overlooking them is the Town Hall, originally built in 1767 as a market house.

It is not intended to be a structured photographic narrative of the area, nor a guided tour, but a kaleidoscope of images from Scrabo Country that hopefully will enable it to be seen through new eyes and appreciated for its charms – a bit of country worthy of the name.

Of course the contrast between the rock-capped hill, with Country Park protection for its ever changing wooded western slopes, the drama of its quarried cliff faces, its panoramic views and great crowning tower, and the gentle spreading farmlands around it, gives Scrabo Country a unique dimension.

Suddenly it's spring and full steam – or rather diesel – ahead to get the land ready for the year's crops.

It also tells the story of a landscape shaped by desert winds where the dinosaurs walked, earth's deep fires, marching ice and finally the hands of men over 7,000 years of farming.

Man's hands worked the land but the land did not just grow his crops; it grew the people too – generations of them. It is our common heritage – our shared environment.

It is a richly endowed land; with an average of 270 growing days a year it's well-drained fields of glacial clays

The patterns of the earth's richness.

The flat reclaimed vegetable-growing lands along Strangford Lough's northern shores are among the most productive in Ireland, supplying the populations of Belfast and the other towns in North Down – and elsewhere through the major super-market chains.

One of the costs of successful, expansive farming has been the paucity of woodland in Scrabo Country. It now occupies a little over 1 per cent of the land, the only two significant areas being Killynether Wood on Scrabo hill and the plantations around the lakes at Kiltonga Nature Reserve in Newtownards, both of which are islands of rich diversity of plant and bird life. All the other patches of venerable woodland are the remnants of planting schemes around

and sands are fruitful. An above average percentage of the land (for Northern Ireland) is arable and the annual rotation of fields between cereal, vegetables and pasture create the ever changing patterns and textures that are such a feature.

Farming is generally on a large scale with farm buildings widely separated across the patchwork of arable fields. The patterns of the farmed landscape began with the plantations of the 17th and 18th centuries with new tenant-farmers clearing land and dividing it up with hedges and woodland. From the late-19th century owner-occupation of farms spread and over the next century, with the most successful farmers buying out their neighbours, the size of holdings increased.

great houses dating from the 18th and 19th century. Fortunately most of our boundary hedges were planted long before the advent of the devastating flail and other industrialised methods of hedgerow management so many of their trees, oak, beech, sycamore and ash, got to grow to maturity and now survive to stand tall and often majestic along the roadsides.

The enlargement of fields since the 1960s through hedgerow and ditch removal to facilitate the increasing mechanisation of farming, and the increasing monoculture of perennial ryegrass for grazing have also resulted in a diminished habitat for wildflowers and wildlife, although thankfully hedge grubbing has not been as extensive as in many other areas of the British Isles.

Baaa – humbug.

Hedges are an important – in fact an indispensable – heritage feature and can be said to define the character of the landscape, and nowhere more so than in Scrabo Country, rising and swooping as they do over the drumlin curves. Most of today's hedgerows date from before the middle of the 19th Century during the decades of the field enclosures. They are vital feeding grounds and shelter for insects and flocks of sparrows, redwings, fieldfares and finches as well as corridors for animal movement. Two thirds of our native bird species nest in hedges.

The rural environment has changed so much over the past century as farming has evolved in response to changing technologies, demands and opportunities. It would be hard to predict what changes lie ahead during this century. The economies of scale that can come with 'factory farming' in response to the ever-increasing

When in 1744 Donegal landowner and businessman (of Scottish extraction) Alexander Stewart used the dowry that came with his new wife to buy the extensive neighbouring manors of Newtownards and Comber he also bought a small estate a few miles down the Strangford coast and built a cabin on a drumlin as a week-end retreat – with a fine view of the hill at the heart of his new demesne and surrounding townlands. Today the estate is Mount Stewart, one of the finest stately homes and gardens in the British Isles – and the view, now with the distinctive tower built a hundred years later, remains to be enjoyed.

downward pressures on consumer prices and therefore production costs have been perhaps the major driving force but the backlash against it because of what is seen as its unacceptable effect on our environmental heritage that is increasingly appreciated and valued – by farmers themselves as much as anyone – hopefully will restore and maintain a balance.

The lessons we learn, the lessons we teach, the examples we set today will determine what kind of landscape will be there for our descendents. Everyone who knows what there is to be found and enjoyed in our countryside today will know that it is worth cherishing and protecting.

Colourful spinnakers bring festive colour to the waters of Strangford Lough during the race season.

A dramatic sky moment above Strangford Lough.

There is one spectacle grander than the sea; that is the sky

Victor Hugo

The Book of Time

For Godly spires and men's towers,
For the gentry's stately bowers,
For stout brown walls
To define their acres
Of curving drumlined landscape.
In a thousand years
Of splitting, drilling, prising,
Carting away and sculpting
Iron-capped Scrabo Hill's
layers of warm soft stone,
The Book of Time was opened.

A million pages, written in sand,
Each one a testimony
To be read in the quarried cliffs,
Of deserts without end, crystal grains
Piled and patterned by the winds
And churned by torrents
from far-off mountain heights
Even as they themselves crumbled,
And continents danced their dance
Across ballroom earth.

Gaze on these bastions now, with wonder
At their story – buried deep, raised high,
Rent and split by the rupturing crust,
Exposed but saved from marching ice
By armour forged in earth's deep fires
Today falcon, raven, jackdaw
Circle and soar – and nest on ledges
Once the sand their ancestors,
Triassic's beings, walked and
left their marks on.

David Kirk

A fine crop of cabbages ready for the market.

Left behind in the soil after last year's harvesting two potatoes survive and flower like jewels among a field of sprouts.

Newtownards Model Primary
School (formerly the National
Model School), a fine example
of the many elegant buildings
constructed over centuries using
sandstone from the 'hill next door'.

Time and vandalism
have reduced
this abandoned
farmhouse to
a sad ruin.

Early autumn dew bejewels a spider's web spun to catch insects visiting a Crocosmia blossom near Scrabo's quarries.

**Those who dwell among the beauties
and mysteries of the earth are
never alone or weary of life.**

Rachel Carson

April and the glorious gorse
shines like the sun itself as the
tilled fields wait to be planted
with the new year's crops.

Patches of winter vegetables
create a multi-coloured
geometric tapestry across
the drumlins' curves.

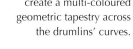

Strips of polythene pattern the spring landscape – they advance the germination and young growth of the crops by a few weeks, adding a significant premium to the prices they fetch in the marketplace.

Summer grazing for a troop of horses on the hills overlooking the Dundonald and Lagan valleys.

It had been there for more than 3000 years before the invading Vikings came. They called it the *Kempenstane* (Big Stone); today the Kempe Stone, or the Greengraves Dolmen as it is 'officially' known, stands as a reminder to those who now work the land of the farming heritage they are heirs to.

Rosebay willowherb
flames with summer
exuberance.

Keeping vigil
over a promising
young crop . . .

Autumn colour
flares through
Killynether wood.

Still winter, but the colour is spreading along the gorse hedges that define the patterns of the landscape.

Whitewashed farm buildings bring a distinctly Continental touch to a piece of countryside in the shadow of Scrabo hill.

If the sight of the blue skies fills you with joy, if the blade of grass springing up in the fields had the power to move you, if the simple things in nature have a message you understand – rejoice, for you soul is alive.

Eleanora Duse

Dark bands across the high cliff walls of Scrabo's South Quarry show where surging magma, solidifying to the form of basalt known as dolerite, forced its way between the strata, baking and bleaching them to a lighter colour than the sandstone's 'natural' browns, oranges and purples.

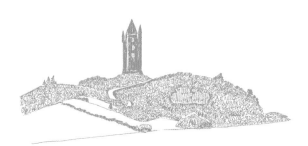

Sculpting Scrabo Country

Four hundred and thirty million years it took to build, shape and reshape, and finally gentle the landscape that is Scrabo Country.

It is the creation of all those endless millennia with their dramas of tectonic upheavals, of continents colliding and being torn apart again, of cold ocean depths, of high scorched deserts, of mountains of ice grinding away ancient rocks before melting away leaving deep rich soils where a new wave of life would come to spread and flourish – with man adding the final touches.

It could be claimed in fact that Scrabo Country was the birthplace of farming in Ireland! The oldest known Neolithic site on the island, containing remains of man's first domesticated animals, was found beside Ringeill Quay, just six kilometres south of Scrabo Hill. It's age was calculated at 6,200 years.

Finds of late Mesolithic flint implements at sites all round its shores reveal that for the previous 2,000 years Strangford Lough had fed generations of hunter-gatherers who fished its rich and sheltered waters and hunted the endless woodlands that clothed the hilly lands around. The bay-filling inter-tidal mudflats that characterise the upper lough now would not then have been anything as extensive.

Whether it was they who took up and learned the new 'settled' farming ideas spreading across Europe or a new wave of Neolithic colonisers brought them is not known (it was probably a mixture of both) but the process began of changing the spreading forests of elm, oak, hazel and alder – and the peaty swamps that filled the hollows between the drumlins – to pasture and tillage. The result is the landscape of today.

The soils the first farmers cleared and cultivated had been waiting for them for 7,000 years, left to blanket the eroded solid rock surfaces – stiff clays and fine sands dropped by the melting ice and moulded into little drumlin hills, and stretches of well-drained gravels spread by the torrential rivers of glacial melt-water, especially along the valley of today's Enler River (the Dundonald Gap geologists call it). It was the end of the last period of glaciation, known as the Late Midlandian, which lasted from 23,000 years ago to 13,000. The alignment of the drumlins show that the ice flowed from the direction of Lough Neagh, although there are some older drumlins left by earlier ice advancing southwards from Scotland.

But this was only the final phase (so far!) of nearly two million years of long glacial episodes with grinding ice sheets sometimes higher than the Mourne Mountains,

Low morning sunlight and the immaculately straight furrows of the skilled ploughman highlight the patterns of the ice-moulded drumlin landscape south-west of Scrabo Hill.

Ice and water produce an elegantly shapely landscape.

Geology may be looked upon as the history of the earth's changes during preparation for the reception of organized beings, a history, which has all the character of a great epic

Edward Forbes

alternating with shorter warm spells such as we enjoy at present and which sculpted the solid bedrocks and created the setting and scenery of Scrabo Country.

It lies between the arms of two ridges of the ancient hard rock that underlies most of County Down, the Silurian greywacke, once seabed of the ancient Iapetus Ocean that was turned to rock in the collision of the American and European continents 430 million years ago. Today's broad Dundonald valley floored with Triassic sandstone hides a more dramatic one carved out of the Silurian rock – a borehole west of Scrabo Hill passed through more than 1,500 feet of sandstone and dolerite before reaching the bottom!

And of course this Triassic sandstone is the rock virtually synonymous with Scrabo. Although it underlies the north end of Strangford Lough as far south as Greyabbey, the Dundonald Valley and the Lagan Valley from Whiteabbey to Lurgan it rarely appears above the layers of glacial till and soil and it is its 'exposure' from nearly a thousand years of quarrying Scrabo Hill for great building works that has given it iconic status.

It is not known how thick the sandstones were at their maximum but staining of the Silurian rock show that they once were almost as high as the Craigantlet hills, filling the Dundonald Valley.

They were formed at a time when for 40 million years Scrabo Country was located in the interior of the 'super-continent' Pangea, formed when all the earth's land masses were fused together in one. It was at the present latitude of north Africa, a vast area of scorched desert building huge thicknesses of wind-blown sand from mountain ranges being eroded far away and occasionally swept by torrents that brought flash floods and even temporary lakes, evidence of which can be seen in the form of layers of mudstone. Life was sparse but hardy pre-dinosaur creatures obtained a living – and sometimes left their footprints in the sands, still preserved. Worm casts and those of fresh-water shrimps can also be found.

But it was 150 million years after the last of the sandstone layers were laid that the event happened without which there would have been no Scrabo (or much else of the north of Ireland's most distinctive geology). As North America began to pull away from Europe, giving birth to the Atlantic Ocean, the same tectonic convulsions that created the granites of the Mourne Mountains and the Giant's Causeway basalts were trying to force deep magma up through the thick sandstones too. It failed to reach the surface but the pressure split the rock between the horizontal layers deep down and surged in to harden as 'sills' of dolerite, some a few inches thick, others hundred of feet.

One of these, now almost 200 feet thick, but probably originally thicker, provided the armour plating that protected the sandstone below it from the grinding ice – it survived to form Scrabo Hill while all the rock around was eroded away.

The Butterlump Stone, an unmistakable landmark on the shore five kilometres south east of Scrabo Hill, is an excellent example of a glacial erratic – a giant block of dolerite from the surface of the Hill transported by the ice and dumped on the sandstone that had been ground away to a much lower level.

**A stone is ingrained with geological
and historical memories**

Andy Goldsworthy.

Underlying all of Scrabo country, in fact most of County Down, but overlaid in places by younger limestones and sandstones, is the ancient, hard and fine-grained Silurian gritstone known as greywacke laid down more than 400 million years ago as seabed near the South Pole. It's hardness makes it the most important rock in the country for road-making and concrete constructions – it is even exported to England – and many quarries dot the countryside. One of the biggest is this one at Ballystockart, west of Comber

Nature is a vast tablet, inscribed with signs, each of which has its own significancy, and becomes poetry in the mind when read.

Hugh Millar

It is barely half a century since the quarrymen cut their last block of Scrabo sandstone but nature has wasted no time in clothing the bare rock of the South Quarry's cliffs with colourful garb. Too much too quickly, complain the geologists who like nice clean stone to study.

These layers, or sills, of iron-hard dolerite rock now cap Scrabo Hill, the hill they helped create by protecting the soft sandstone below them from millennia of glacial erosion that lowered all the countryside around. But the hundreds of feet thickness of sandstone that was above these sills when they were formed was eroded away over nearly 60 million years

Stones have begun to speak, because an ear is here to hear them. Layers become history and, released from the enchanted sleep of eternity, life's motley, never-ending dance rises out of the black depths of the past into the light of the present.

Hans Cloose.

Flaming willow-herb makes a bright skirt for the walls of layered sandstone – layers laid down long before the earth had flowers to put a smile on its face.

We may observe in some of the abrupt grounds we meet with, sections of great masses of strata, where it is as easy to read the history of the earth, as it is to read the history of Man in the archives of any nation

Jean DeLuc.

Close-up showing how sharp is the junction between the sandstone and the dark dolerite (this can be studied not far along the path from the south quarry to the north).

Ripple marks on this boulder beside the path between Scrabo's two quarries, similar to those seen on any beach today, show that similar forces were in action when water flooded across the Triassic sands more than 200 million years ago.

More than two hundred million years ago a flash flood swept across the desert sands and left a layer of mud. It dried, shrank and cracked under the sun and its cracks were filled with more wind-blown sand creating patterns that can often be seen preserved on blocks of Scrabo stone.

Today mud –cracks just like them can be seen in fields flooded and then dried – however these cracks will not be filled with desert sands!

The porous structure of Triassic sandstone makes it one of the most important groundwater sources anywhere. Although now supplied with water from the Mourne Mountains and a state-of-the-art treatment facility, the distinctive circular reservoir at Ballycullen (created originally in the early 19th century to supply Newtownards Workhouse, now the Hospital) was originally fed by horizontal tunnels drilled through the depths of the sandstone, one of which was almost a mile long!

Of Walls and Men

Walls,
Stitching the patchwork
of the human landscape,
Their stones resting
in crafted beds,
Print-outs
that recount the sagas
of a world's long story.

Walls,
Defining limits
Defining lives,
Their stones
coaxed from the living rock
or salvaged
from the glacial jetsam.

Walls to follow – or to stop
and lean upon;
To touch, to feel
and wonder at the past
their stones tell of.

Walls,
The heritage of men,
Their stones the heritage of earth.

David Kirk

Drivers heading towards Scrabo Hill from the south would hardly notice them as they passed between two short stone walls on Moate Road. There are the parapets of a bridge built in 1850 across a cutting for the new Newtownards section of the Belfast & County Down Railway line from Belfast to Donaghadee. Scrabo sandstone was perfect for the structures needed for the expanding railway networks and tens of thousands of tons were quarried for this purpose.

Centuries of headstones form ranks like a congregation of the faithful before the walls of the Grey Abbey. Built for the Cistertians in 1193 it is the oldest building of known date to use carved Scrabo sandstone in its construction, showing that the qualities of the stone have been recognised and quarried for great building works for almost a thousand years.

Angled sunshine throws the high walls of Scrabo Tower into relief, highlighting the differences in which the quarried dolerite blocks protrude. The window frames and other 'ornamental' features are carved from sandstone.

Locally, one of the biggest Scrabo Stone structures was Comber Spinning Mill, built by the Andrews family in 1863-64. Dominating the town and the local economy, it provided livings for thousands of local people until it closed in 1997. It is now a complex of luxury apartments. The Andrews name is of course also renowned through that of Thomas Andrews Jnr. chief designer of the ill-fated Titanic, who died with his ship. The Andrews-Titanic Walking Trail around Comber is now a popular tourist attraction for the area.

Presiding with elegant dignity over Conway Square, the heart and centre of Newtownards, what has been described as Ulster's finest Georgian Town Hall was built of Scrabo stone in1767 as a market house. It now also houses the town's Arts Centre. Time took a toll of the stonework and in the 1990s it was skilfully refaced using stone from Ballyalton Quarry to the west of Scrabo Hill. Below this quarry there is a 430 feet thick sill of dolerite and the heat of this bleached and hardened the stone above it making it more durable than the red or brown stone originally used for the building.

Unfortunately now in the middle of a busy road junction with road signs and other such hardware for company, the most venerable piece of Scrabo heritage, The Market Cross, is the only one of its kind and age in Northern Ireland. Originally built in 1636 it fell prey to the great destroyer Cromwell in 1658 but was rebuilt in 1666 and probably used as a shelter for the town's night watchman. The stonework (even its roof) has survived the centuries better than some, .

St Mary's Church in Comber, another stately example of Scrabo stonework.

A Symphony in Sandstone – St Patrick's Roman Catholic church in Newtownards was built in 1875-77, paid for by Lady Londonderry.

Scrabo provided the stone for arguably the most elegant of the Newtownards churches – St Mark's.
Built in 1817 it underwent a complete make-over a few years ago with the stonework cleaned and
repaired. The spire was a later addition, of stone from a different source, and darker than the original.

Dig deep for the earth's riches!

When the April wind wakes the call for the soil, I hold the plough as my only
hold upon the earth, and, as I follow through the fresh and fragrant furrow, I am
planted with every foot- step, growing, budding, blooming into a spirit of spring.

Dallas Lore Sharp.

Spring

L ate March, take your rest on the bench seat at the high path viewpoint on Scrabo Hill and cast your eye over the multi-coloured patchwork of fields spreading to the Mourne mountains and clothing the Dundonald Valley to Belfast. Listen carefully and you can almost hear the lovely countryside yawning and stretching as it and the life it bears begin to waken from their long winter sleep.

Soon the landscape patterns will change as new growth bursts and spreads along the hedgerows and over the pastures and fields and the ploughs get others ready for another year's crops. Furrows are exquisitely carved in sympathy with the contours of the land and, as Seamus Heaney said, 'the turned-up acres breathe'.

Closer to hand the top of the hill will soon blaze with the brilliant yellow clouds of gorse bursting out over its rocky outcrops and spreading down its quarried cliffs.

A flock of sharp-eyed gulls take a break from their usual seafood diet from Strangford's waters to forage for whatever pickings the plough turns up.

Killynether Wood below your feet will froth with the first bright green of new spring leaves which gradually create a sunshine-harvesting canopy over the swathes of bluebell and wood anemone, celandine and primrose below.

Shame to spoil this work of art by growing plants in it!!

A strip of last year's brassicas that have gone to flower along the edge of a field ready for a new planting create a bright band of colour.

A wealthy landowner cannot cultivate and improve his farm without spreading comfort and well-being around him. Rich and abundant crops, a numerous population and a prosperous countryside are the rewards for his efforts.

Antoine Lavoisier

The air and the earth mingled in the warm gusts of spring; the soil was full of sunlight and the sunlight full of red dust, the air one breathed bore earthy smells and the grass underfoot had a reflection of the blue sky in it.

Peter Loewer

43

The leaves are barely on the trees but already
the new year's crops are thrusting upwards.

Polythene sheets
to accelerate plant
growth bring back a
look of winter to the
late spring fields.

– A very well-ordered field!

A faint green flush colours
the tilled fields as the first
new shoots seek the light.

**The green things growing, the green things growing,
The faint sweet smell of the green things growing!**

Dinah Craik.

45

The low-lying flat lands between the Newtownards-Comber road and the sea are among the most productive and important vegetable producing areas in Northern Ireland.

New spring – new life and rich grazing

**All I want is to stand in a field
and to smell green, to taste air, to
feel the earth want me, without
all this concrete hating me.**

Phillip Pulfrey.

Home comforts!

**Whoever needs milk
bows to the animal**

Yiddish saying.

Dandelions in full spring bloom turn the central reservation of the dual-carriageway between Newtownards and Dundonald into a river of gold.

Gorse rolls like a wave across the pastureland.

**Roses are red,
Violets are blue;
But they don't get around
Like the dandelions do.**

Slim Acres.

Patterns

The Landscape Artist

To the artist a fine brush,
The sculptor a honed chisel,
The poet a (reluctant) pen,
The farmer – a plough.

For the artist his canvas,
The sculptor his stone,
The poet his blank sheet,
The farmer – his field.

Working the fruitful earth,
Sharp blades caressing, opening it,
Freeing the spirit of the soil
with timeless craftsmanship

On the hedge-stitched patchwork,
Tended by the generations,
Straight furrows cradle his crops
in patterns of fresh new life.

Man, machine and the living palette,
Tuned to the rhythms of creation,
Creating a kaleidoscope
of wonderful landscape artistry

David Kirk

Lines of new life patterning the spring fields in this montage show the skilful artistry of the ploughman – straight as a die from hedge to hedge – except where a fairy thorn has to be accommodated!

Fringed with its coronet of spring gorse, Scrabo Hill commands views from the Mountains of Mourne in the south to the Antrim hills north – and on a clear day to the western highlands of Scotland and the Lake District. Comber nestles in the river plain at the east end of the Dundonald Valley down which a great ice sheet once ground its way.

– A spread for the eyes,
a feast for the spirit

James Macnamara

The Hill that Commands

E ven without its monolithic tower Scrabo Hill would have a commanding presence in the North Down countryside, rising steeply with wooded slopes at the head of Strangford Lough it stands with benign authority over the towns, houses and fields and the fruitful drumlins clustered around its skirts like children.

With its tower it is an iconic landmark for miles around, visible even from Slieve Donard and the Scottish coast.

The decision in the mid-1970s to create a protected parkland for all to enjoy by combining the rocky dramas of the quarried hill with the colourful, ever-changing woodlands of Killynether was an inspired one, creating a diverse yin-yang world – an entity where the whole is greater than the sum of its elements.

The Hill's 500 feet hard stone summit, still armour-plating the depths of warmer softer sandstone beneath, commands views that on a clear day can range from Ailsa Craig to Cumbria to the Mournes and to Slemish Mountain. Beneath your feet stretch the waters of the Lough, the Ards Peninsula and the multi-patterned rich farmlands spread out all around. Climb the Tower's 140 feet and the panorama is even more breathtaking.

The main entrance to Scrabo Country Park. Turn left from the car park at the top of this road to be in charming Killynether Wood, turn right for the Hill, the Tower and the quarry paths. Other entrances are from Killynether's own car park or up the quarryman's track from the Old Belfast Road on the outskirts of Newtownards.

The walk from the car park to the summit and the tower skirts Scrabo Golf Club's scenic 18-hole course in gently rising smooth tarmac with unfolding views to the south and east (it's also a brilliant sleigh run when the snows come!). Halfway up a path, onwards from a little picnic site to the right leads to the start of the dramatic quarry walk about 300 feet below. Another way down is a steep rough path through the bracken and gorse from just north of the tower; it's steep in places and can be slippery after rain.

This sculpture greets visitors to the car park – reflecting the water movement and marine life of Strangford Lough spreading out in full view below.

It is Scrabo's varied physical environments and the diversity of habitats they offer, that fill it so full of interest and opportunity to pursue a range of interests from birdwatching to plant hunting to photography and of course just plain walking and enjoying family activities. The quarries have been designated as Areas of Special Scientific Interest. Unfortunately the uncontrolled spread of vegetation that covers much of the quarry floors and walls is making the study of the hill's geological features increasingly difficult. Two chomping herds of feral goats used to help contain the vegetation but they were not deemed compatible with public park requirements.

But stand on Scrabo Hill and you are not looking just at delightful scenery – you are looking back over 5,000 years of continuous human history – Scrabo (the word means 'rough cow pasture') has been a hive of activity and habitation through all man's time in Ireland. .

Rising above the swamps and forests that would have been the landscape of early man, but on the edge of the rich feast of seafood that Strangford Lough offered, Scrabo Hill was a natural place to set up home and evidence in the form of flint implements has been found of even early Mesolithic hunter-gatherer occupation there.

Neolithic and early Bronze Age man followed and left his traces in the form of arrowheads, scrapers and knives but it was the late Bronze Age and early Iron Age peoples who really left their marks – hut circles scattered all across the hilltop. Mostly embedded in the manicured swards of the golf course, sadly, following successive centuries of cultivation and landscaping they are virtually undetectable to the untrained eye. Several hut enclosures – groups of huts within a surrounding bank have also been identified and it is believed that Scrabo Hill hosted one of the biggest communal settlements in Ireland of the time in Ireland.

The summit of the hill is also believed to have been enclosed by an Iron Age fortress wall which may have been in use for more than a thousand years.

One feature that is clearly visible on the golf course fairways is the pattern of cultivation ridges or 'lazy beds' possibly dating from famine times when desperate attempts to grow potatoes brought every square inch of cultivatable ground into use.

Spring – and massed bluebells come into their own, seeming to reflect the joyful blue sky above. Beyond Newtownards the low hills of Whitespots Country Park and Clandeboye rise above the horizon.

Early morning light brings a chill glow to the Comber River estuary.

Few golfers enjoy such dramatic surroundings
as those of Scrabo's 18-hole course ...

... weather permitting!

**I've spent most of my life golfing
– the rest I've just wasted**

David Kerr

Scrabo's Towering Glory

For many people of course Scrabo IS the great tower rising nearly 150 feet above the hill; now almost defining the identity of this part of County Down. Built of the same stone on which it stands the Tower seems to almost be growing almost as an organic extension of the very hill itself.

Its three feet thick walls are built of rough-hewn hard dolerite blocks cut from the hill below it with embellishments of sculpted sandstone and it stands on the site of an ancient stone circle – traditionally known as the royal seat of the King of the Fairies –

with an air of solidity and permanence that reflected the social self-confidence of its time. Such sites have usually been imbued with religious significance and even today a Christian service is held there every year on the morning of Easter Sunday. The land was in fact owned by the Dominican Orders until the dissolution of the monasteries in the 16th century.

When the 3rd Marquis of Londonderry, of Mount Stewart, died in 1854 after a distinguished military and diplomatic career (and whose descendents still own Scrabo Hill and much of the land around) his widow wanted to create a memorial that would leave no doubt about his stature – no one was to be allowed to forget him! A hilltop tower was decided on and the design brief stipulated that 'size and mass were the chief objects'. She certainly achieved her aim. (We will

The stately tower crowns Scrabo Hill, truncated by the great cliffs of the South Quarry but sloping down across the golf course, with its rocky outcrops, to merge with the cultivation-patterned landscape beyond.

gloss over the common myth that the Tower was paid for by his tenants, grateful that he did a lot for them during the famine, neither of which happened).

Built to a design by the leading architect of the time Sir Charles Lanyon at a cost of £3000 – his much more flamboyant original design had to be reined back to reduce the cost – construction started in 1857.

Whatever its story today the Tower is to be enjoyed not just as a uniquely dramatic, if quirky, landscape attraction but as the irreplaceable focal point of the Country Park, and it has proved a valuable tourist attraction for the area.

Even before the creation of the Country Park, the Tower was a popular attraction, with the three Millin sisters – granddaughters of its first tenant and caretaker, a quarry foreman who brought up eight children in it! – running a small tearoom. After they left in 1966 the Tower's structural condition was found to have deteriorated and it took a massive programme to restore it to a safe condition, including stonework restoration, roof repairs, lightning conductors – and putting in two additional floors (which had been omitted during construction to cut costs). This created rooms that now house the Country Park wildlife and geology exhibition and an audio-visual facility.

While sadly at the time of writing (May 2014) the Tower has been closed to visitors for an indefinite time, normally it is open every day during the summer and on Sunday afternoons the rest of the year allowing people to enjoy the 'adventure' climb up its steep 122-step stone spiral staircase to the 'battlements' and

soak in the stunning views of a 360 degree panorama, enhanced by informative display panels. Hopefully this exciting experience will be available again soon.

Montbretia
provides patches of
exciting colour.

A field of 'wild' sunflowers offer
an exotic touch to the view
from below the south quarry.

Fuchsia
aflame by the
trackside.

Earth laughs in flowers

Ralph Waldo Emerson

Autumn colours suffuse the bracken and
trees on the east slopes of the hill

The pair of Peregrine falcons, for many years exciting residents
of Scrabo's high ledges, have now gone, but many other
species make their home there, an environment providing
ideal conditions for small mammals and insects to feed on.
The croaking of nesting ravens is a common sound – here
one flies across the high cliff face of the North Quarry.

Only its footprint has been found on Scrabo's
sandstone but it was enough for experts to identify
and reconstruct the creature that made it 250
million years ago. Chirotherium it is known as,
an archosaur, predecessor of the dinosaurs.

A Scrabo Flashback

As a teenager in the 1950s I would often mitch off from school rugby or cricket afternoons and cycle from Dundonald along the narrow switchback that was the 'old' road to Newtownards (now levelled and widened to be the dual carriageway) to the Scrabo quarries looking for fossils and unusually marked stones. In those days, not long after quarrying had more of less ceased and two herds of goats kept the vegetation in check, you could clamber over the scree slopes of quarry waste right up to the base of the soaring cliffs and explore along them. You could also scramble up from the north end of the quarry to the edge of the golf course and walk along the cliff tops. Now the goats have given way to bramble, gorse and Health and Safety dictats, and adventures to gentle rambles – but with more than enough pleasant compensations in the scenery and plant and bird life.

At other times the Misses Millin, who still lived in the Tower – the third generation of their family to act as caretakers – serving visitors with tea and scones with cream made from goats milk, would allow two or three of us to 'camp' in their little corrugated iron washhouse which was in the steep hollow just behind the Tower and we could enjoy Primus stove dinners and moonlit views of the Lough and the spreading landscape.

Scrabo Tower offers an exciting opportunity for young people who want to take up the adventure challenge of abseiling down its height of almost 150 feet – and an opportunity for charities such as Marie Curie to raise funds by organising well-managed sponsored abseiling events such as the one pictured here

The Stone That Shaped Men's Lives

The taking away of 12 million cubic metres of its layered sandstone certainly changed the shape of Scrabo Hill – and it also shaped much of surrounding landscape created by man.

Steep faces of a beautiful white, pink and dark red stone, accessible, easily split, shaped and carved, was the stone worker's dream, and over almost a thousand years it was eagerly 'devoured' for building homes and walls and creating some of the most elegant buildings man created for his gatherings and worship, not just in the neighbouring towns, villages and farms but across much of Ulster and as far away as Dublin and even, it is reputed, New York.

By the time quarrying had ended in the early 1960s an estimated 12 million cubic metres of rock had been cut away from the north and south faces of the hill, leaving more than a mile of almost vertical rock faces up to 50 metres high in places. The intrepid walker, leaving the tracks (and negotiating some dense vegetation), can come across other small workings, possibly marking the first cutting of the stone, which could have been from where stone was taken for the first known building works such as Grey Abbey (1193) or the 12th century Holywood Friary.

Quarrying, which involved the splitting of stone into blocks by driving steel wedges – plugs and feathers – between the layers would have expanded to meet the needs of a growing population and local builders and farmers took full advantage of having such an ideal stone on their doorstep. It was appreciated elsewhere too, being carted to Dublin and elsewhere 'in great abundance' (William Montgomery, 1683). By the middle of the eighteenth century is had become an important industry with a number of companies operating quarries, the most important of which was the one opened in 1826 by Robert Corry who went on the found the building supplies firm that still bears his family name.

But it was the industrial revolution of the mid-nineteenth century with the burgeoning construction of factories (such as the huge spinning mill built in Comber by the Andrews family), the building of churches and homes to cater for growing urban populations, and perhaps above all the arrival of the railways which transformed the transport of cut stone, that really took extraction to a new level, with steam-powered mechanisation and a tramway linking the two quarries and down to a specially constructed railway siding at Newtownards.

The surge in production created hundreds of jobs with skills being passed down through generations with some families actually living in the quarry complex. However changes in building technology, the availability of cheaper sources of sandstone and also an increasing difficulty in cutting back into the hill safely led to a gradual decline during the 20th Century. Production had virtually ceased by the end of the Second World War and the South Quarry finally closed in 1966.

Quarrying of Scrabo Hill finally ended after a thousand years with the closure of the South Quarry in1966. Now the cascading gorse shows how nature is reclaiming the bare stone cliffs.

The visitor track winds under the
soaring walls of the North Quarry.

The drama of the cliff faces left
by the extraction of 12 million
cubic metres of stone.

This straight-sided 'portal' was cut through the rock to allow extraction from the expanding north quarry. It now marks one end of the visitor path through the quarry.

One of two old bridges, crossing tracks to even older quarry workings north of the North quarry, were used to carry down stone when the working levels were higher up the hill.

Late June, and Scrabo Country reaches the
full exuberance of summer growth.

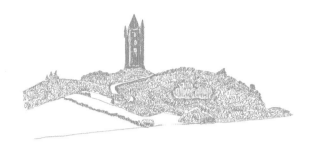

Summer

If spring is the time of exciting anticipation, summer is the time of rejoicing. The fields and their hedgerows, the roadside verges, the trees, young slips and venerable sages, are throbbing and bursting with life eager to get their year's work done in the few short months our climate gives them.

The frolicking spring flowers have snuggled away for another year but where the sun can shine have made way for their showier successors – buttercups, daisies, speedwells then foxgloves, willowherbs, thistles, ragworts. In the high trees and low verges insects flourish at different stages of their development, providing rich pickings for the myriads of small birds feeding themselves and their young.

Walkers now throng the paths of the Park enjoying nature's show, golfers pit their skills and enjoy the scenery and on the Lough the overwintering birds have

The poetry of the earth is never dead.

John Keats

given way to sailors, canoeists, wind-surfers enjoying the challenges of the waters and winds.

All in all – plenty to rejoice about!

Landscape west of Scrabo Hill. The tall brick chimney is a reminder of when many of Co Down's field carried a different crop – flax and helped many avoid the worst consequences of the potato famine which hit this area hard. The Unicarval mill itself was demolished long ago.

Plants cry their gratitude for the sun in green joy

Astrid Alauda

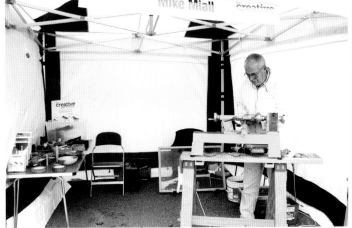

Every Saturday Conway Square in
Newtownards becomes a true market place
and hums with activity as people come
to browse round the open air stalls.

One of the big events every summer in
Newtownards town square is the Craft
Fair which gives local crafts people
the chance to demonstrate their skills
– and visitors the chance to admire
and acquire pieces of their work.

The mix of vegetables, grain and grazing
creates a banded landscape under Scrabo Hill.

A land of mixed farming
among the drumlins!

The Shaping

Mountains moved across the land.
Mountains of ice, hard as the rock
Of Down's floors of ancient
Seabed grits and desert sands.

Recycling earth's past.

Freezing and melting, surging and shrinking,
Splintering, crushing, churning,
They reduced stone to fragments,
They moulded a new landscape.

The landscape of the drumlins

Earth mother's tender breasts,
Snuggling soft together,
Swelling in curves so gentle,
They call for your embrace

A land renewed, bearing new life.

Men came. They cleared their slopes,
Lined them with hedge and furrow,
Learned to win the bounty
Of the fruitful soils.

To feed their many generations.

David Kirk

It is dry, hazy June weather. We are more of the earth, farther from heaven these days.

Henry David Thoreau

A scattering of silage bales wait to be gathered up and stored for winter feeding.

Summer Sunday afternoons and people come from afar to Comber Square with their camping chairs to enjoy the music of silver and flute bands. Comber Square might well be called 'The Square of the Heroes'. Overlooking the square and all that happens in it from his 55 ft column is the statue of the town's hero general, Rollo Gillespie, who was actually born in the Square in 1766. An outstanding warrior in the armies of King George III he was killed in Nepal in 1814 reputedly uttering the immortal words 'One more shot for the honour of Down'. Below him in height if not in honour is the soldier who commemorates the local men who died fighting in the First World War. The Square's gardens themselves were created as a memorial to those who gave their lives in the Second World War.

July and the main-crop potatoes are in full bloom.

The changing face of farming. Why just grow vegetables and sell them to processors when you can move to the next level and process them yourself to the finished ready-to-eat consumer product which this pioneering company has successfully done.

A countryside that just has it all!

Summer makes a silence after spring.

Vita Sackville-West

Harvest time at
Ballyhenry

Harvest patterns
the landscape

**Plants give us oxygen for
the lungs and for the soul**

Linda Solegato

This handsome fellow waits to greet visitors
at the Ark Open Farm near Newtownards.

. . . and this one keeps a
sharp eye on things!

The cow is nothing but a machine which makes grass fit for us people to eat

John McNulty

The yellow of the gorse and broom have long faded but cyclists on the Comber Greenway now enjoy the lilac glory of the willowherb. The Greenway runs for seven miles along the route of the old Belfast & County Down Railway line between the east of the city and Comber providing a traffic-free route to be enjoyed by walkers and cyclists.

Local Orange lodges bring music and colour to Newtownards every Twelfth of July as they parade through the town on their way to the buses that will take them to the North Down demonstration, held at a different venue each year.

Late summer and the landscape mellows towards autumn.

Earth Laughs in Flowers

A flock of hoverflies get stuck into the goodies in the bloom of a lesser dandelion.

A puff of wind takes the first flying seed from this dandelion head.

Rich pickings for the hedgerow birds as
hawthorne and bramble fruit ripen.

A thistle seed-head
bursts upon the world

Wild poppies greet walkers by the Comber Greenway …

… And others
laugh by a
field verge

**May all your weeds
be wildflowers**

John Bennett

A glorious spread of rosebay willowherb provides
a colourful backdrop to a wild parsley

A colourful
congregation of
wild flowers crowd
the roadside bank

**God loved the flowers and
invented soil. Man loved the
flowers and invented vases.**

Marshall Boyd

Daisies laugh in the summer sunshine

Raindrops hang
glistening from
the stems of these
montbretia.

**Spring unlocks the
flowers to paint the
laughing soil.**

Reginald Heber

As the Seasons Roll Round

The ever-changing landscape – a series of pictures of the same piece of farmland showing the variety of scenery it can present over the course of a couple of years as it bears different crops in rotation.

Dawn light from across Strangford Lough shines
through the boughs of the bare winter trees.

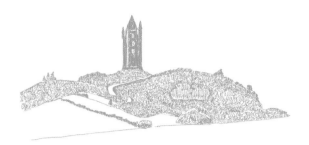

Killynether Wood

For those who love to walk with the companionship of noble trees, in their spring freshness, summer majesty, autumn sublimity or winter nobility Killynether Wood has it all to offer – and more!

All the more valuable in an area of pastoral landscape with patches of mature woodland few and far between. With almost 30 species of trees from sky-scraping beech, pine and oak planted 150 years ago to younger rowan, hazel and holly and a varied under-storey of shrubs and flowering plants it has an enchanting diversity.

The main entrance to Killynether wood from its car-park.

And with a bonus that many such woods don't enjoy – the 1.5 mile 'circuit' of its 45 acres takes the walker not just between the trees and through the extensive hazel wood, with its springtime carpets of bluebell and wood anemone, but along its high skyline, where you brush shoulders with the crowns of the giant trees, end enjoy

views stretching to the Belfast hills and the Mourne Mountains.

The older among us can remember the Victorian Gothic pile, Killynether Castle as it was known, built in 1858 on the flat grassed area west of the former walled

Autumn-tinted Killynether spreading round the east face of Scrabo Hill.

of beech. The south-westerly aspect of the steeply sloping ground encourages vigorous growth.

A wide variety of flowers can be found in the woods and among the hazel plantations (which are regularly coppiced and enjoy high light levels). Celandine, wood sanicle and wood sage, sheep's sorrel, cuckoo pint, greater stitchwort and even orchids are there to be enjoyed.

Bird life too is rich and varied – robin, stonechat, tree creeper, magpie, chiffchaff, spotted flycatcher, linnet, redpoll and the long-eared owl have all been recorded. And although they try to stay out of sight, foxes. stoats and badgers make their homes there.

garden. Although an integral part of the Country Park Killynether is actually owned by the National Trust, to whom it was donated in 1937 by Helen Weir who was born in the house. At that time is was used as a Youth Hostel, and the estate was requisitioned by the Army at the start of the Second World War (car parking there now is on the concrete foundations of the military Nissen huts). It had a series of uses after the war but deteriorated to such an extent that it was decided to demolish it in 1966.

Killynether is a carefully managed park, with the venerable trees, now well past their normal life expectancy, being carefully monitored and reduced to a safe height if deemed necessary. As well as plantings of new trees to replace in time the fallen ones, there is an unusually prolific natural regeneration especially

At the west end of the lowest section of the Killynether walking track you can see the remains of a section of a 'wall and ditch' structure – this was built sometime in the seventeenth century, and ran all the way round the base of Scrabo Hill. It is believed it was built to enclose 500 acres of deer park, but who built it is not known.

Of Moss

Furry bonnet for stumps and stanes,
Living shroud for the fallen mighty
as they slowly melt back into the earth-mother's womb

Mossy carpet spreading brightness
across the sombre woodland floor
splashing the colours of life across a dark canvas

David Kirk

Who could resist exploring this enticing hillside
track through the rocky heights of Killynether.

The tall trees
seem to invite
the walker to
join them.

**And this our life, exempt from public haunt,
Finds tongues in trees, books in the running
brooks, Sermons in stones, and good in everything.**

Shakespeare

Beech, the 'Queens of the Woodland' dance in their bright spring greenery.

Bluebells clamber joyfully between the rocky outcrops in the heights of the wood.

For in the true nature of things, if we rightly consider, every green tree is far more glorious than if it were made of gold and silver.

Martin Luther

93

This wonderful depiction of woodland life, with all the features carved by chain-saw in the shape of animals and birds, enchanted visitors to Killynether for years – until decay and a strong wind brought the tree trunk it to the ground in 2012.

A man does not plant a tree for himself; he plants it for posterity.

Alexander Smith

Going to the woods is going home.

John Muir (1838-1914).

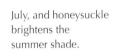

July, and honeysuckle
brightens the
summer shade.

The fulfilment of autumn
brings out the ultimate
glory of the woodland

A drifting autumn mist
brings a monochrome
day to the woods.

Golden leaves
carpet the steps into
the woods from the
main car park.

**Falling leaves hide
the path so quietly.**

John Bailey

96

Snow transforms the woodland floor.

A light snowfall
dusts the bare
branches.

Like a lake of blue waters a field of leeks laps a colour-changing hedgerow.

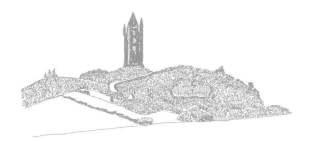

Autumn

Autumn bursts into flame.

Autumn – nature's grand finale, the fulfilment of another year's husbandry as crops are gathered in, the fulfilment of another year's growth, fertilisation and new life, the fulfilment of another year's busy photosynthesis producing growth for hedge and woodland giant.

The days shorten, temperatures slide – time to call it a day before the weather turns nasty; hibernation calls. The chlorophyll that turns leaves into chemical factories and gives us the world of green woodlands breaks down leaving other chemicals to take the stage – and giving the leaves their glorious autumn colours – yellow orange and red – as they cascade down turning the world to gold and giving us the exuberant colour climax of the year to enjoy.

The farmed landscape changes too. The hedgerows and their scattered trees bare their structures to the winds, some fields are left to rest before the next season, others tilled in preparation. Insect life retreats to the ground, the music of the birds fades and life snuggles down.

Autumn – The season for enjoying the fullness of life – partaking of the harvest, sharing the harvest with others, and reinvesting and saving portions of the harvest for yet another season of growth.

Denis Waitley

This year's crops harvested
the fields can rest awhile.

It was one of those perfect autumnal days which
occur more frequently in memory than in life.

P D James

Furrows of fruitfulness.

Low autumn sun shines through the usually sombre leaves of a fine crop of sprouts coming on nicely for Christmas.

Thy bounty shines in autumn unconfined And spreads a common feast for all that live.

James Thomson

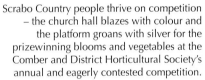

Scrabo Country people thrive on competition – the church hall blazes with colour and the platform groans with silver for the prizewinning blooms and vegetables at the Comber and District Horticultural Society's annual and eagerly contested competition.

...and competition is also fierce in beak and claw when hundreds of birds from around Northern Ireland are brought together at the Andrews Memorial Primary School every autumn to battle for cherished rosettes at Comber Cage Bird Society's Open Show.

"Autumn is the eternal corrective. It is ripeness and color and a time of maturity; but it is also breadth, and depth, and distance. What man can stand with autumn on a hilltop and fail to see the span of his world and the meaning of the rolling hills that reach to the far horizon?

Hal Borland.

The grain garnered, lines of straw lead the eye to Killynether and Scrabo hill as they lie drying and wait to be baled.

Straw bales await collection at Unicarval.

Come to us, Lord of Harvest
Teach us to be thankful
for the gifts you bring us

Roy Barton.

Aftermath of harvesting a good cabbage crop.

Autumn
rains can
make life
difficult!

The first autumn blush suffuses this venerable beech.

**The leaves fall, the wind blows, and the
farm country slowly changes from the
summer cottons into its winter wools.**

Henry Beston

A late silage cut near Greengraves.

I go about looking at horses and
cattle. They eat grass, make love,
work when they have to, bear their
young. I am sick with envy of them.

Sherwood Anderson.

Autumn and the football season gets under way. The superb and extensive facilities of the Billy Neill Soccer Centre of Excellence created by Castlereagh Borough Council give teams without their own playing fields, and especially young people, the opportunity to learn and develop their skills. It also offers the only place along its seven miles that people travelling by car, such as those with prams or wheelchairs or their dogs, have safe off-road parking to access the Comber Greenway.

The excellent 'clubhouse' of the Billy Neill centre looks across the landscaped grounds to this scenic lake with its resident swans and other waterfowl.

Gateways

Nothing adds character to a farmed landscape than the variety and ingenuity of 'barrier solutions' that farmers come up with to define and defend their property. And often they survive long after their usefulness has ended. This montage shows some of the bright and practical ideas – and some that are worthy of heritage status!

For decades this field made do with
a redundant telegraph pole as a
barrier – but look at me now!

It is almost exactly 200 years since Lord Londonderry built floodgates and an earthen dyke along the most northerly section of the Lough shore to reclaim 200 acres of saltmarsh and turn it into productive farmland. Over subsequent decades the dyke was extended to more than three kilometres turning hundreds more acres behind it into rich arable fields. The first kilometre of the dyke, the most exposed to south-westerly seas, was armoured at the beginning of this century with massive blocks of stone. Along most of the rest of the way it runs inland from the actual shoreline and the force of waves is dissipated by swathes of saltmarsh.

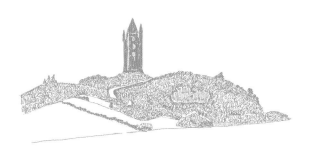

Land and Lough

I t seems only fitting that the richly productive farmlands of Scrabo Country should embrace and protect the headwaters of one of the most biologically rich and diverse sea loughs in Europe.

Now recognised internationally for its importance as a marine habitat – it is the biggest Marine Nature Reserve in the United Kingdom and designated an Area of Outstandng Natural Beauty – Strangford's shores also carry the memories of human life in Ireland from its earliest time.

Looking down on it from Scrabo Hill the Lough stretches south from the flat lands it itself created, its waters curving from sight on the horizon, sometimes, when full tide fills it, shining mirror-bright from shore to shore, at others a pattern of textured mud-flats and water. In the distance its smoothness broken by the sprinkling of small islands and 'pladdies' as they are called, small piles of rock that are the remains of drowned drumlin hills eroded away by the action of the waves.

And it is this wave action, over 15,000 years, washing away the sands and clays from the shores and islands, that has created the huge area – almost 30 square kilometres including the many little bays and backwaters round

Along with the stately Hill and the patterned farmlands around it, the upper reaches of Strangford Lough complete the triumvirate of scenic exuberance that is Scrabo Country. Like a protective rampart the Mountains of Mourne fill the southern horizon.

the shore – of mudflats spreading down from the head of the lough. Rising waters, with the prevailing winds from the south-west behind them, carry more particles in than the turning tide takes away again, so the muds accumulate and build – added significantly to by the millions of cubic metres of material carried down into the lough over the millennia by the rivers draining the glacial till-covered hills around.

Here, in the Dundonald valley, after rising high up on the Craigantlet hills north of Stormont, the Enler River is a tree-lined tranquil stream. Joined a short distance later by the Ballystockart River, which with its tributaries drains the southern slopes, it is the main drainage channel for the valley and grows in strength. Passing through Comber, it takes the town's name and creates a wide estuary, finally meandering through the Lough's salt-marshes and mud-flats. It's flow of fresh water into the lough is second only to that of the Quoile at the southern end.

In fact, think about it – the silts and sands that spread across the Lough and nurture the incredible richness of its life were once the same soils that now grow the crops and feed the cattle of Scrabo Country's agricultural richness!

An amazing 40 per cent of the Lough's total seabed is exposed to the air at low water and while it may look pretty barren from the shore it teems with life – an estimated 1,500 invertebrate species live in, on or under the Lough's diverse seabed environments – the

basis for the rest of the diversity of life the Lough supports, in its deeper waters further south and around the complexity of its shoreline.

Although at the top of the food chain, and the popularity stakes, despite congregating in their tens of thousands, numerically the birds make up a tiny fraction of the lough's varied life forms.

Best known, and undoubtedly the best 'tourist' draw, the pale-bellied Brent goose, almost the entire 30,000 world population of which fly from Arctic Canada every winter to descend on Strangford and feed on the eel grass growing on the mudflats, has become an international icon of the Lough's wildlife diversity.

But the variety of food available – eel grass, algae worms, shrimps, shellfish, even grass in the adjacent fields which the whooper swans enjoy, means that a huge range of wildfowl and waders are catered for – in winter the lough can host 15 different species of each. Barnacle and greylag geese are the biggest of the visitors but wigeon, ducks, knots, plovers, dunlin, oystercatchers, godwits and many more can be seen feeding along the tideline as it comes and goes. When tide is fully in great flotillas of as many as 10,000 birds can be seen floating and resting offshore waiting for it to turn.

The sheltered Comber River Estuary, and a narrow strip along the head of the Lough, constitute one of the few significant areas of salt marsh remaining in Ireland. Salt marshes are a rich nutrient store for the Lough and of great importance in terms of ecology and diversity of plant and non-vertebrate life. They are an important food and shelter resource for wading birds and wildfowl and breeding sites for waders, gulls and terns.

The mudflats spreading across the head of the Lough glow in the first light of a winter dawn. Soon the tens of thousands of wildfowl and waders will get stuck in to another day of feeding on their riches.

In the mud and scum of things
there, always, something sings

Ralph Waldo Emerson.

The Newtownards dyke that protects these fields provides a popular venue for walkers and cyclists.

A gull takes a break on this sign at Patton's Marsh, an area of salt marsh on the seaward side of the dyke walkway.

The mudflats are nothing if not diverse in what can turn up there!

Strangford's Tale

Once upon a time in County Down
A bloody great hole appeared
as earth dynamics pulled a continent apart.

The Newtownards Basin the learned call it,
A thousand metres deep they say it was,
A hundred million years it took to fill it in.
Deep new oceans laid the first layers
with the endless generations of their dead
(Quarried Espie now their quarried tombstone)

The lands convulsed and heaved,
Mountains rose – and were reduced to crystal grains,
Grains that blew and washed and filled the hole.

They buried too all the ancient plains around
under layered depths of desert sands,
which yet more ages turned again to stone.
New oceans came – and left again,
New beings came, had their time – and went.
The continents continued their tectonic waltz.

Strangford Lough stretches to the horizon
in this view from Scrabo Golf Club.

Deep magma split and veined the rocks,
Glaciers came, ground them down and shaped them
Fire, ice and time gave Down its inland sea

Passing oceans now surge in to visit,
Spreading to refresh the richly silted bays
and caress the gentled slopes of fruitful hills,
Where Ireland's first farmers tended the first herds
Where man's new future took hold,
By the shores of Strangford Lough

David Kirk

Shafts of light break through an
overcast sky above Chapel Island.

The tide rises round
the remains of an old
jetty near Castle Espie.

**In still moments by the sea life seems large-drawn
and simple. It is there we can see into ourselves**

Rolf Edberg

Once long ridges of boulder clay in the post-glacial landscape before it was 'drowned' by rising waters, Island Reagh and Island Mahee, linked to each other and the mainland by causeways, are the biggest of the Lough's many islands. The circular site of ancient Nendrum Monastery can be seen at the near end of Nendrum.

Twice a day high tides cover the meandering causeway from the car park at the popular venue of Island Hill at the mouth of the Comber River estuary to Rough Island, an isolated remnant of the post-glacial raised beach – and one of the richest Mesolithic and Neolithic sites anywhere. In the 19th century coal barges unable to get up to Comber berthed at the island and wagons brought their cargo ashore over the causeway.

For many years this totem pole sculpture at the start of the Rough Island causeway celebrated the coming of the Brent geese every year from Canada and the close connections between the area and that country. Sadly time and decay took their toll and it had to be removed in 2013.

To stand at the edge of the sea, to sense the ebb and flow of tides, to feel the breath of a mist moving over a salt marsh, to watch the flight of shore birds that have that have swept up and down the shore line of the continents for untold thousands of years, is to have knowledge of things that are as nearly eternal as any earthly life can be

Rachel Carson

A solitary Glasswort grows on the mud among the strands of eelgrass that draw the thousands of brent geese and other wildfowl every winter.

The Lough's most
famous visitors,
Brent geese from
northern Canada,
fly in to overwinter
and feed on the rich
supply of eel grass

They crowd the
waterline wing to
wing as they feed on
the eelgrass exposed
by the receding tide

Little Feehary Island produces a rich
harvest – for the table and the eye!

At one time under water,
these fields offer good grazing
and wide open spaces.

The yachts of Whiterock, the 'sailing centre' of Strangford, seem to swarm across the water. Little Braddock Island on the left and Sketrick Island on the right, with its fringe of highly desirable shore-side residences, help create sheltered moorings

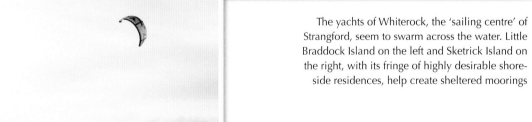

Strangford has been a paradise for generations of sailing and kayaking enthusiasts – and a new sport has entered the scene more recently, as windsurfers dance with the music of the winds and waves.

Christmas – and Conway Square in Newtownards
is ready for the festive cheer.

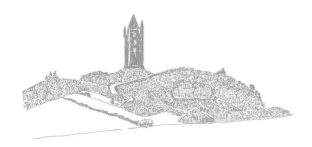

Winter

Winter – the sleeping, when time and life in the countryside seem to stand still. When wind and rain and cold prevail across the subdued earth and the bare boughs. But there can be a bright, pearly quality of light in the winter skies not matched in any other season especially before dusk and after dawn which can bring an element of magic. At no other time can bare trees look more dramatic than against this backcloth.

A quiet day on Scrabo golf course!

Sadly changed climate patterns have meant fewer days now where winter puts on its equivalent of spring colour and autumn drama – a good fall of snow to blanket the land and trees and crunch beneath your feet. For those whose farm chores have to be carried on regardless it may be a pain, but for those who can tramp the roads or explore the Park it creates a winter wonderland.

And you have the knowledge that in the cold earth below the snow dormant plant and seeds lie waiting – waiting for spring to let them burst into life again.

The first fall of snow is not only an event, it is a magical event. You go to bed in one kind of a world and wake up in another quite different, and if this is not enchantment then where is it to be found?

J.B. Priestley

Bright sun and deep snow behind Scrabo hill.

Snow and the Comber Greenway becomes a different world.

Stately sentinels wait patiently for the spring.

There is a privacy about winter which no other season gives you. In spring, summer and autumn people sort of have an open season on each other; only in the winter, in the country, can you have longer, quiet stretches when you can savour belonging to yourself

Ruth Stout.

Winter makes a sharp eye essential
for finding enough to live on.

Flooded fields
and mist make
for a dismal
sort of a day!

**Winter is nature's way
of saying 'Up yours'**

Robert Byrne

Harvesting that Christmas favourite the
Brussels sprout can be chilly work!

Fortunately
this crop of
Brussels sprouts
got harvested
before the rains
turned the soil
to a quagmire.

**January is the quietest month. ... But
just because it looks quiet doesn't
mean that nothing is happening. The
soil, open to the sky, absorbs the
pure rainfall while micro-organisms
convert tilled-under fodder into
usable nutrients for the next crop
of plants. The feasting earthworms
tunnel along, aerating the soil
and preparing it to welcome the
seeds and bare roots to come-**

Rosalie Muller Wrigh.t

133

Killynether's tall trees keep any heat the sun might have off the frozen roadway.

– A solitary lone bare ash crowns a hill near Dundonald.

The russet of lingering autumn leaves the only colour in an icy landscape.

Near Dundonald the soil produces a different crop from the fields around – Christmas trees.

I wonder if the snow loves the trees and fields, that it kisses them so gently? And then it covers them up snug, you know, with a white quilt; and perhaps it says "Go to sleep, darlings, till the summer comes again.

Lewis Caroll

Emergency rations!

A flock of visiting swans come ashore for a forage in the fields near Island Hill.

If winter comes, can spring be far behind?

Shelley

Winter chill whitens the ground and swans, geese and duck seem to huddle together for comfort at Kiltonga Nature Reserve on the outskirts of Newtownards.

It may look pretty but a frozen Kiltonga brings problems for some!

Built in the Twelfth Century on the site of one of Ulster's most important early churches (destroyed by the Vikings) Movilla Abbey fell victim in 1572 to Brian O'Neill's scorched earth rampage. Unlike other such buildings Movilla was not restored by Hugh Montgomery but its grounds have been used for almost a thousand years as a cemetery.

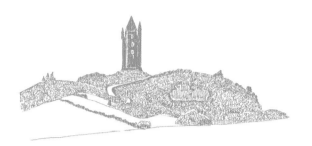

Their Heritage, Their Pride

Fire and ice, two of nature's great forces, laid the foundations of Scrabo Country's landscape but it was two of man's most powerful driving forces, inspiration and enterprise, that shaped the human landscape we know today – defined its character and laid the foundations of its cultural, agricultural and economic riches.

In fact Scrabo Country was the heart of the area that witnessed the birth and evolution of arguably one of the most important events in the defining of the whole future of the Province of Ulster – indeed Ireland itself; what has come to be referred to as the Dawn of the Ulster-Scots – people, principles and heritage.

'Founding fathers' of the Ulster-Scots were the heads of long-established Scottish families – the Montgomerys and the Hamiltons.

Although near neighbours in Ayrshire James Hamilton and Hugh Montgomery had little in common – except that they had both achieved positions of considerable influence at the court of James VI of Scotland, who in 1603 became also James I of England – and overlord of Ireland. Hamilton, whose father had been the first Protestant Minister in the town of Dunlop, was a noted academic and 'agent' (ie spy) for the king – and Hugh

Montgomery, who became Sixth Laird of Braidstane on the death of his father was an aristocrat and soldier who had fought in the army of King William I of Orange.

Flashback 30 years to the 'war' between Sir Brian O'Neill, the most important chieften in the north of Ireland whose territory covered most of Down and Antrim, and Queen Elizabeth I. Out of favour at court and with much of his land requisitioned for a 'plantation' of English peasant settlers (which failed) O'Neill decided in 1572 that if he couldn't have his estates the English weren't going to and so he embarked on a 'scorched earth' programme across North Down, and Ards burning down all the buildings that might be of use to English invaders. These included Grey Abbey, Newtownards and Holywood Priories, Movilla and Comber Abbeys.

A couple of years later the troublesome Brian was captured and executed and ten years after that the lands had passed to his grandson Con who astutely worked his way back into Royal favour. However a lethal altercation with some English soldiers in Belfast landed him in prison in Carrickfergus Castle – and it was in this that the seed of the Ulster-Scots heritage was germinated.

Newtownards Priory the first building to be restored by Montgomery. He doubled it in size and built the bell tower. He and many of his successors are buried there. The Priory stands at the edge of what is known as the Rose Garden, a peaceful haven occupied by the War Memorial, which until 1636 was the town's centre and market square. Immediately next to it is the former Castle which he restored as his family home, 'Newtown House'

Grey Abbey, the first Gothic-style building in Ulster, was built by the Cistercian order in 1193. Burned by O'Neill in 1572 it was re-roofed by Hugh Montgomery in 1607 and served as a parish church for the new Ulster-Scots settlers until 1778. It is now in the care of the Environment and Heritage Service

The main entrance door to the Priory, bearing the Montgomery coat of arms.

Con's wife, Ellis, got in touch with Hugh Montgomery and offered him a deal – if he could 'spring' her husband from goal and use his influence to get him a royal pardon she would give him half of her husband's estates.

To Hugh, who already shared a growing interest in developing the Irish 'colonies' this was a Heaven-sent opportunity. He succeeded in his side of the bargain but before the deal could be signed fellow-Scot Hamilton stepped in. He convinced the King that it wouldn't be a good idea to give Montgomery that amount of land; it should be divided three ways, he said – with himself getting the third part!

For the rest of their lives the two men co-existed in what has been described as a state of 'mutual hatred' but they were above all practical businessmen so they co-operated in the division of the lands and their ambitious plans for their settlement and development. Hamilton got three separated swathes of land – North Down, the centre of the Ards Peninsula and an area stretching from Comber to Killyleagh, still the family home of his descendents. Montgomery got an equal area of land, 'sandwiched' between Hamilton's estates. Rosemount at Greyabbey is still the Montgomery home.

There had been a number of costly but failed attempts to 'settle' the lands of Ulster during the 1500s so the King was glad to go along with a plan by Hamilton and Montgomery to settle north and east Down, at their own expense, not with the usual army of peasants but by inviting already successful Ayrshire farmers, some large estate owners, often with their tenant-farmers,

and their families, and the craftsmen and skilled artisans, and professional people necessary to build a society. It could probably claim to be the first PPS – Public Private Sector partnership!

They had tens of thousands of acres of good land to offer their followers as viable-sized farms at affordable rents. Naturally the response was enthusiastic; it is estimated that over the next few decades at least 10,000 people took up their offer.

When one looks across today's Scrabo Country landscape, it's well-ordered fields rich with grain, vegetables and pasture it is hard to picture what has been described as the 'wasted, depopulated and desolate' countryside left by O'Neill which met the first immigrants and on which they settled down to build their new homes. Many must have felt like getting on the next boat home!

According to the Montgomery family records *"In the springtime, Anno 1606 those parishes were more wasted than America. Thirty cabins could not be found, nor any stone walls, but ruined roofless churches, and a few vaults at Gray Abbey, and a stump of an old castle at Newtown, in each of which some gentlemen sheltered themselves at their first coming over".*

The first settlers sailed from Portpatrick to Donaghadee in May 1606. They included most of the Montgomery and Hamilton extended families and a number of Montgomery tenants. Hamilton made his home in Bangor, Montgomery in Newtown (it became Newtownards later). The first settlers were given lands around Newtown, Bangor and Donaghadee and as numbers grew so did other towns with Comber, Killyleagh, and Greyabbey becomming centres of population and development.

Those who signed up to take on big swathes of land were expected to build substantial stone homes. Their sub-tenants, as an eye-witness wrote: 'made temporary shelters of sods and saplings of ash, elder and birch trees with rushes for thatch and bushes for wattles'.

Life was precarious. Survival must have been touch and go for several seasons but nature was kind to the new settlements and their first crops were bounteous which gave them time them to get their roots firmly established. Of immense help too was the untiring dedication of Hugh Montgomery's wife Elizabeth who was hands-on in her management of the settlements. She ensured that the settlers had the tools and equipment they needed, built watermills and textile mills, giving birth to new linen and woollen industries. Importantly she also established Newtown as a market town which attracted a constant stream of traders from Scotland.

Montgomery himself set about repairing the major buildings destroyed by O'Neill – Newtown Castle and adjacent Priory (he added the tower that is still there) and Grey Abbey, where he installed a Scottish minister. He also built schools and a sports centre in the town and he and Hamilton repaired or rebuilt more than 15 churches across their lands.

Hard work and the community spirit that bound the new settlers paid off – their farms flourished, their towns grew and as the word spread of the success of the project the flow of new settlers became a flood,

bringing their Scots traditions, culture and religion with them. Later a period of religious antagonism in Scotland brought a wave of dissenting and Presbyterian ministers who did much to cement the faiths of the settlers.

So successful was the Montgomery-Hamilton project that is became the model for the colonisation of Virginia in 1607, the plantation of six more counties of Ulster in 1610 and the settlement of Nova Scotia in 1621. In 1622 Montgomery became first Viscount of the Great Ardes and Hamilton first Viscount Clandeboye.

It was the inspiration and leadership of the Montgomery and Hamilton families that eventually led to the development of today's Scrabo Country landscape, but it was the resolution, resilience and determination of the Ulster-Scots people themselves which transformed the wasted desolation into a unique symbiosis of people and land, often in the face over the centuries of great economic, social and religious difficulties.

The full fascinating story of the settlement of Scrabo Country, 'The Dawn of the Ulster-Scots', and the events leading up to it, and its consequences, can be found in the publications of the Ulster-Scots Agency (a number of which are available from the Ards Tourist Information Centre in Newtownards) and its website – www.ulsterscotsagency.com. The Hamilton and Montgomery Manuscripts, the family records, are available on CD Rom.

A shroud of silent stillness for the ancient burial ground beside Gilnahirk Presbyterian Church, which dates back to 1787.

A Legacy of Names

Ballyhaft, Ballyblack and Ballyharry,
Ballyreagh, Ballyskeagh and Ballyhenny,
Pieces of a townland jigsaw that is the Ards
with names – of those who shaped the lands
or of the works they left behind.

Names that ring like poetry;
Lasting echoes of the long forgotten.
Ballyalicock and Ballywatticock

Quarried Ballyalton, Ballycullen too
Crossnamuckly, Ballyaltikilligan,
Greengraves where great stones
the mark of those went before.
Ballymagreehan, Ballybarnes and Ballystockart ,
Cunningburn, Gilnahirk, Craigantlet.

A cacophonous catalogue of heritage and history.

David Kirk

Cottage

Publications

For more information and to see our other titles, please visit our website
www.cottage-publications.com
or alternatively you can contact us as follows:-

Telephone: +44 (0)28 9188 8033
Fax: +44 (0)28 9188 8063

Cottage Publications
is an imprint of
Laurel Cottage Ltd.,
15 Ballyhay Road,
Donaghadee, Co. Down,
N. Ireland, BT21 0NG